COWBOY

BY ROBERT KLAUSMEIER
ILLUSTRATIONS BY RICHARD ERICKSON

LERNER PUBLICATIONS COMPANY
MINNEAPOLIS, MINNESOTA

The American Pastfinder series is produced by Lerner Publications Company
in cooperation with Greenleaf Publishing, Inc., St. Charles, Illinois.

Design by Melanie Lawson

Klausmeier, Robert (Robert C.)
    Cowboy / by Robert Klausmeier ; illustrated by Richard Erickson.
        p. cm. — (American pastfinder)
    Includes index.
    ISBN 0-8225-2975-0
    1. Cowboys—West (U.S.)—History—Juvenile literature. 2. Ranch
life—West (U.S.)—History—Juvenile literature. 3. Cattle trade—West
(U.S.)—History—Juvenile literature. 4. West (U.S.)—History—Juvenile
literature. I. Erickson, Richard (Richard W.) II. Title. III. Series
F596.K589 1996
636.2'13'0978—dc20   94-38347

Manufactured in the United States of America
1 2 3 4 5 6 - H - 01 00 99 98 97 96

CONTENTS

Introduction

The cowboy is one of the most celebrated heroes in American history. He broke wild mustangs, rounded up herds of fierce longhorn cattle, and drove them north on long and hazardous trail drives. He built the sprawling cattle empires and helped open the great American West to settlement. Through courage, skill, and endless hours of exhausting work, the cowboy forged himself a lasting place in history.

American legend paints the cowboy as a hard-riding, hard-drinking, sharpshooting hombre who tamed the Old West from the back of his faithful horse. And that is how he appears in countless books, pictures, songs, and movies. This image contains a kernel of truth. But it tells only part of the cowboy's story.

The real story isn't always so glamorous, but it is heroic. For the brief time they rode the range, cowboys cast a big shadow. To this day, they capture qualities of freedom, strength, and individuality that shape our national personality.

THE COWBOY ERA AND THE CATTLE EMPIRE

The golden age of the cowboy was only a tiny slice of American history. It lasted about 20 years—from the end of the Civil War (1865) until the mid-1880s. By that time, bad weather, worn-out pasture lands, and dropping cattle prices had forced an end to the open range. Cattle had to be raised on fenced-in ranches. English Herefords replaced the wily Texas longhorns, and the legendary cowhand became a simple ranch hand. But the roots of the cowboy's story go back to a much earlier time.

The Beginnings of Cattle Ranching

In about 1769, Spanish missionaries arrived in the Mexican territory of California. They brought with them small herds of domestic cattle, which thrived in the grassy valleys of California and the lower Rio Grande. Before long, the missionaries were teaching Indians as much about handling cows as about Christianity. From the Spanish came the techniques of herding on horseback, roping, and the roundup.

When Mexico broke away from Spain in 1821, Mexican ranchers, the West's first real cattle barons, seized the missionaries' ranges. Indian and Mexican cowhands (*vaqueros*) went to work for the ranchers.

When the United States fought Mexico in 1846, Mexican troops retreated south of the Rio Grande, leaving the ranches open to any taker. Rustlers stole and slaughtered off cattle by

the thousands. The herds recovered decades later, and Texas became the center of the American cattle industry.

With the Civil War, western cattlemen joined the army, leaving herds to run wild. After the war, returning soldiers slapped brands on the nearest animals and went into the cattle business. The era of the cowboy began.

From Cimarrons to Texas Longhorns

The early Spanish cattle were narrow-faced, stringy, and able to survive any type of weather. These animals were known as *cimarrons*, or "wild ones." They raised themselves. Their meat was tough; mostly they were sold for their hides. The cimarrons were later crossbred with American and French stock. The results were Texas longhorns, huge cattle with a horn-spread of four, five—even seven—feet.

Grazing Land

The sweeping plains from Canada south to the Rio Grande and from Kansas west to the slopes of the Rockies were known as "the Great American Desert." Annual rainfall averaged less than 20 inches, and the area was considered unfit for farming. But the plains were covered by remarkably nutritious grass. At one time this gigantic range fed more than 40 million buffalo. But in the years following the Civil War, the buffalo were slaughtered ruthlessly.

Meanwhile the grass continued to grow—offering rich grazing for any animal that could survive the harsh climate. The animals came from Texas: hardy longhorn steers.

In the space of 20 years—from 1867 to 1887—about 10 million cattle were driven north through the grassy plains. These great cattle drives brought money, merchants, and settlers to an area long considered worthless. Cowboys made it possible.

Cow Country

Texas was the place where American cattle ranching began, and herds of Texas longhorns were the first to travel the long trails north to railroad hubs. At rail centers such as Abilene, Dodge City, Denver, Wichita, and Kansas City, the longhorns were loaded on cattle cars for trips to slaughterhouses and markets in the East.

The trails pictured on this map were used by the herds driven to market during the 40 years of cattle drives. Opening in 1840 and heading northeast from Texas to Missouri, the Shawnee was the first major trail to the cattle markets. The best-known and most heavily traveled of all routes was the Chisholm Trail, which handled half the cattle out of Texas.

The Growth of Northern Ranches and a New Breed of Cattle

After the Civil War, great wagon trains of pioneers moved west, bringing farm-raised oxen, as well as milking and breeding cattle. These domestic shorthorns prospered on the western prairies, eventually replacing the fiercer longhorns as beef cattle.

Cattle ranching in Wyoming began in what is today the southeastern corner of the state. Wyoming ranchers had nearly unlimited grasslands on which to expand. They also had access to direct rail transportation (the Union Pacific Railroad opened a shipping center in Cheyenne as early as 1870), so there was no need for the long trail drives. In addition, investors in the East as well as in England and Scotland considered Wyoming Territory to be the most profitable area for raising cattle.

UTAH
TERRITO

ARIZONA
TERRITOR

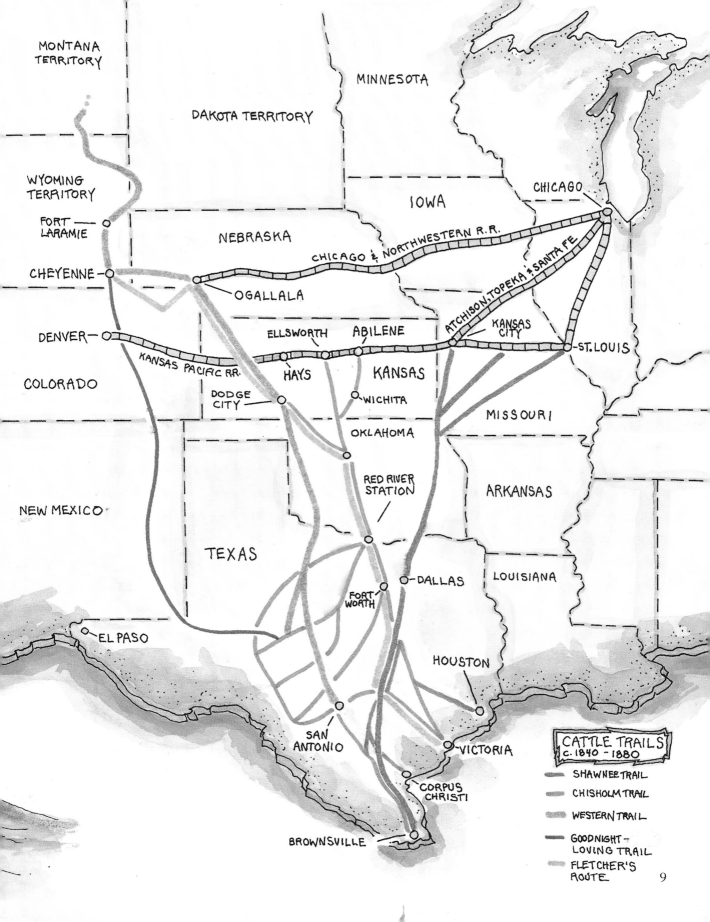

MONTANA
TERRITORY

DAKOTA TERRITORY

MINNESOTA

WYOMING
TERRITORY

CHICAGO

FORT
LARAMIE

IOWA

NEBRASKA

CHICAGO & NORTHWESTERN R.R.

CHEYENNE

ATCHISON, TOPEKA & SANTA FE

OGALLALA

KANSAS
CITY

ELLSWORTH   ABILENE

ST. LOUIS

DENVER

KANSAS PACIFIC R.R.

HAYS

KANSAS

COLORADO

DODGE
CITY

WICHITA

MISSOURI

OKLAHOMA

RED RIVER
STATION

ARKANSAS

NEW MEXICO

TEXAS

DALLAS

LOUISIANA

FORT
WORTH

EL PASO

HOUSTON

SAN
ANTONIO

CATTLE TRAILS
c. 1840 - 1880

VICTORIA

CORPUS
CHRISTI

SHAWNEE TRAIL

CHISHOLM TRAIL

WESTERN TRAIL

GOODNIGHT-
LOVING TRAIL

BROWNSVILLE

FLETCHER'S
ROUTE

9

THE COWHAND

At the center of the thriving cattle industry rode the cowhand. In the twenty-odd years of the cowboy's heyday, some 40,000 cowboys herded cattle across the plains. Most cowboys were young—their average age was 24, and many were still in their teens. This was not a job for the old or middle-aged. Ten years of hard riding was about all the human body could take.

Cowboys came from all walks of life. Some were young veterans of the Civil War. Others came from the East, or even

from England and Scotland, searching for adventure. Tall tales about the daring cowhand multiplied. The myth of the "Wild West" spread throughout the East.

Nearly one in three cowboys was either Mexican or black. The Mexican vaquero was the forerunner and constant companion of Texas cowboys. At the height of the cowboy era, more than 5,000 African Americans worked on western ranches. Texas, the home of so many cowboys, had been a slave state. Before the Civil War, slaves herded cattle and broke horses. After the war, many freedmen put their experience to work as hired hands on Texas ranches.

Indian cowboys also rode the range—especially in Oklahoma (Indian Territory) and the far Northwest. Native American cowboys operated a number of ranches in Indian Territory.

Some cowhands were women—often wives and daughters of ranch owners—who worked the range and took part in the long cattle drives. The successful cowgirls learned to rope, ride, and shoot as well as the cowboys.

Fearless—even reckless at times—the cowboy was also healthy and strong. The exhausting work weeded out weaklings. To strangers he seemed "strong and silent." Among friends the cowhand was talkative and enjoyed rough jokes. Trail cooks played practical jokes such as tying sleeping cowboys' spurs to a log and then rousing them with a call to breakfast. Another joke was to put pie dough in a sleeping man's beard.

A Cowboy's Uniform

In the years just after the Civil War, cowboys wore whatever suited ranch work and the western climate. Clothes were usually dark, woolen, and extra large—for comfort. Over the next 20 years, cowboy clothing was influenced by the vaqueros. By the 1880s, a kind of cowboy "uniform" emerged.

The John B. Stetson hat with a deeper crown and not so broad a rim…took the cake…. High-heeled boots were the rage…the heel was made to start under the foot, for what reason I never knew, unless it was the same motive that prompts the gals to wear the opera heel in order to make a small track.

— Texas cowboy W. S. James

Many cowboys wore buckskin gloves to protect hands from rope burns or rein blisters. Trimmed with beads, quillwork, or fringe, they gave the cowboy a dash of style.

Shirts were dark flannel or cotton pullovers without collars or pockets.

At first, pants were heavy wool, often strengthened with buckskin where they rubbed against the saddle. In the 1850s, Levi Strauss began making denim pants in San Francisco. The pants were so strong they could be used to stuff cracks in bunkhouse walls, mop floors, even tow stranded vehicles.

Boots cost $20 to $30, about a month's wages. Heels were long and tapered to keep from slipping through the stirrup. Toes were tapered to slide into the stirrup— and slip free if the cowboy were thrown. (The most common cause of death was being dragged by a horse.)

The jingle of spurs was music to a cowhand's ears. A light touch of the spurs guided a horse when the cowboy's hands were busy with a rope.

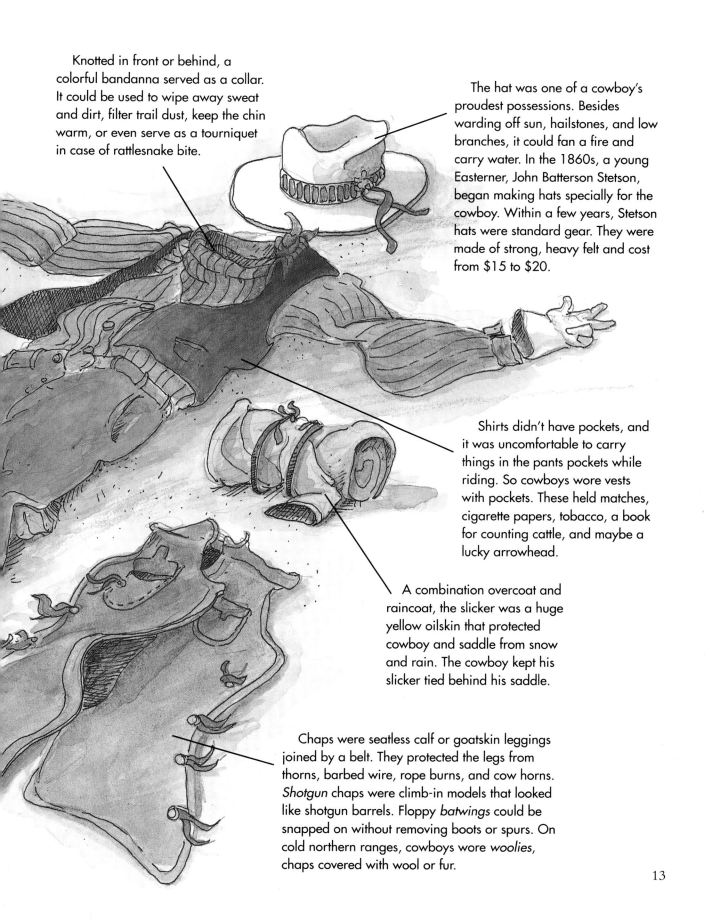

Knotted in front or behind, a colorful bandanna served as a collar. It could be used to wipe away sweat and dirt, filter trail dust, keep the chin warm, or even serve as a tourniquet in case of rattlesnake bite.

The hat was one of a cowboy's proudest possessions. Besides warding off sun, hailstones, and low branches, it could fan a fire and carry water. In the 1860s, a young Easterner, John Batterson Stetson, began making hats specially for the cowboy. Within a few years, Stetson hats were standard gear. They were made of strong, heavy felt and cost from $15 to $20.

Shirts didn't have pockets, and it was uncomfortable to carry things in the pants pockets while riding. So cowboys wore vests with pockets. These held matches, cigarette papers, tobacco, a book for counting cattle, and maybe a lucky arrowhead.

A combination overcoat and raincoat, the slicker was a huge yellow oilskin that protected cowboy and saddle from snow and rain. The cowboy kept his slicker tied behind his saddle.

Chaps were seatless calf or goatskin leggings joined by a belt. They protected the legs from thorns, barbed wire, rope burns, and cow horns. *Shotgun* chaps were climb-in models that looked like shotgun barrels. Floppy *batwings* could be snapped on without removing boots or spurs. On cold northern ranges, cowboys wore *woolies*, chaps covered with wool or fur.

The horn (or pommel) at the front of the saddle served to keep the rider in place, to hold the lariat, and to act as a hitching post for the rope when the cowboy lassoed steers.

HOME IN THE SADDLE

Every cowboy was fussy about his saddle. For months on end, he sat in it all day long—and sometimes half the night. When he turned in after a hard day's work, the saddle became his pillow. A saddle was so important to his life that the expression "He's sold his saddle" came to mean that a man was finished—washed up— as a cowboy.

Unlike a horse, which the boss supplied, the saddle was a cowboy's own property. A typical Western saddle, which weighed 30 to 40 pounds, was made of leather and set on a wooden frame. A good saddle cost about $30—about a month's pay—but it would last for 30 years or more.

The cinch fastened the saddle securely to the horse. It was held in place by a leather latigo, or strap, drawn through rigging rings. The cinch usually was placed directly under the horn. Double cinches helped keep the saddle in place during heavy roping.

The broad stirrups helped the cowboy stand or sit "tall in the saddle" when riding down steep slopes or trotting along the trail.

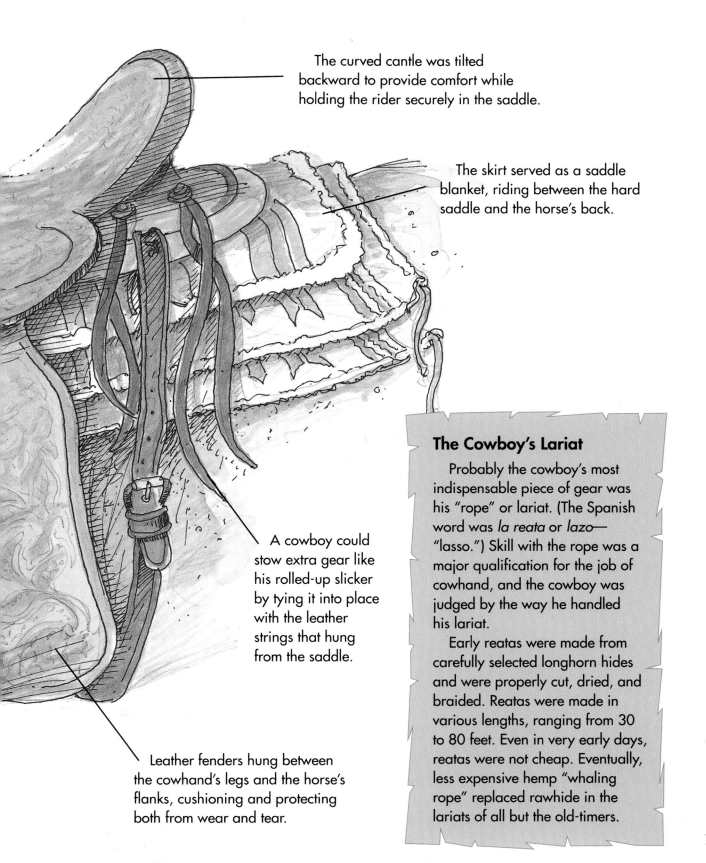

The curved cantle was tilted backward to provide comfort while holding the rider securely in the saddle.

The skirt served as a saddle blanket, riding between the hard saddle and the horse's back.

A cowboy could stow extra gear like his rolled-up slicker by tying it into place with the leather strings that hung from the saddle.

Leather fenders hung between the cowhand's legs and the horse's flanks, cushioning and protecting both from wear and tear.

The Cowboy's Lariat

Probably the cowboy's most indispensable piece of gear was his "rope" or lariat. (The Spanish word was *la reata* or *lazo*— "lasso.") Skill with the rope was a major qualification for the job of cowhand, and the cowboy was judged by the way he handled his lariat.

Early reatas were made from carefully selected longhorn hides and were properly cut, dried, and braided. Reatas were made in various lengths, ranging from 30 to 80 feet. Even in very early days, reatas were not cheap. Eventually, less expensive hemp "whaling rope" replaced rawhide in the lariats of all but the old-timers.

RIFLES AND SIX-SHOOTERS

Oh, a man there lives on the Western plains,
With a ton of fight and an ounce of brains,
Who herds the cows as he robs the trains
    And goes by the name of cowboy.

He laughs at death and scoffs at life;
He feels unwell unless in some strife.
He fights with a pistol, a rifle, or knife,
    This reckless, rollicking cowboy.

He shoots out lights in a dancing hall;
He gets shot up in a drunken brawl.
Some coroner's jury then ends it all,
    And that's the last of the cowboy.

—popular 19th-century song,
"Oh, a Man There Lives"

Despite their gun-toting image in movies and in ballads such as the one above, cowboys seldom carried a gun on the job—although they usually owned one.

The most common use of firearms was for hunting. When a cowboy went after an antelope or jack rabbit for his supper, he took a rifle or shotgun. But large firearms were clumsy to hold and, when carried in a saddle sheath, they rubbed against the horse, producing sores. So hunting trips were usually short.

The Colt revolver was easy to carry but effective only for close-range shooting. It was good for killing rattlesnakes, finishing off a horse with a broken leg, or turning aside a stampede (by firing directly in front of the lead steers).

When not strapped around his waist, the cowboy's cartridge belt and revolver were usually stashed in his bedroll. On long trail drives, bedrolls and guns were stored in the chuck wagon until needed.

Cowboys were aware of the manly image that guns gave them, and they often strapped on their guns when paying a call to a young woman. However, when visiting a cabin or ranch house, they removed cartridge belts and guns and left them hanging on the saddle horn or a nail inside the door. This was etiquette.

Hot-tempered shootouts with other cowboys rarely occurred, but there were exceptions. Despite laws banning firearms in many cattle towns, cowboys sometimes celebrated the end of a trail drive by getting drunk and wildly shooting off their guns.

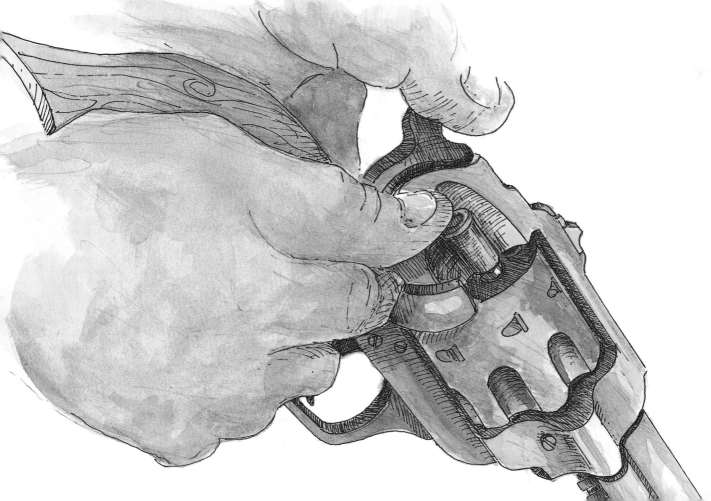

THE COW PONY

The cowboy's most important ally in working cattle was his pony. Ranch owners usually supplied these animals, but they were half-wild, ornery beasts that needed breaking in before they could be used.

Most cow ponies came from the open range. They were wild mustangs (from the Spanish word *mesteño*—"stray") or mustangs interbred with U.S. cavalry mounts or eastern workhorses. The ponies roamed free until they were about four years old. In late spring, cowhands corralled them and set about training them. This work was called bronco busting or breaking, and its object was to break the animals' wild spirit and teach them fear and respect for the cowboy.

The bronco buster first lassoed each pony, tethered it snugly to a post, and slipped the bridle over the animal's mouth (a risky task). Next, the saddle blanket was slapped over the pony's back, followed by a 40-pound saddle. Finally the bronco buster released the pony and leaped aboard. The meaner and rougher a horse behaved, the rougher the treatment it received from the cowboy's whip, spurs, and rope end. The treatment wasn't meant to be cruel; it was simply the quickest way to prepare the horse for work.

Throughout the years, far more cowhands were injured or killed by accidents on horseback than in all the gunfights pictured in western movies and television shows. In a book about his years as a cowboy, E. C. "Teddy Blue" Abbott told of how one morning he watched Bill Charlton, a fellow cowboy, trying to ride a "half-broke horse." Charlton was not a very good rider.

> *The horse cut up some, and Bill got mad and spurred him. At that time they all had these Mexican spurs with long rowels and bells on them, and a long hook—a cinch hook it was called—on top of the rowel; this was to hook into them leather bands, when a horse was bucking, and keep you from being throwed. Now Bill accidentally ran this hook into the cinch ring, and it caught there, and the horse bucked him off. He would have been kicked to death in a minute. I was riding a green horse myself, but I got alongside Bill's horse and grabbed the cheek strap and throwed myself out of the saddle…and got the cinches unbuckled and the saddle off and Bill out of it.*

The horse was a cowboy's constant companion and a vital part of his image. But despite this, the cowboy's attitude toward his pony was less than romantic. He felt about the pony much the way a farmer today might feel

about his truck: show enough care to keep the thing running, but don't waste time pampering it.

There were, however, "special" horses. Every cowboy could tell stories about one favorite horse and its unique habits, skills, or intelligence. And each horse had a name that could be traced to its character or markings, or maybe to an incident in which it had been involved.

A Cowboy's Life

Typically, cowboys signed up to work on a ranch's spring roundup in March or April. Some worked for small family ranches, others hired out to enormous spreads covering more than 200 square miles. When spring roundup was over, the cowhands spent the summer with a trail outfit, driving vast herds of longhorns north along cattle trails to distant railroad towns. Then they returned to Texas for fall roundup in September.

Average cowboy wages were $25 to $30 per month, plus food. Wages were paid in gold and silver coins, which the cowboy carried in a leather "poke" with a drawstring. Some hands managed to save part of their wages and, in time, became ranchers themselves. However, a far greater number headed for town as soon as they were paid and "shot the works" on new duds, gambling, bad whiskey, and entertainment.

Summers on the Ranch

Cowboys who stayed at the ranch had their hands full over the summer. Cattle on the open range often had to be treated for blowflies. These insects laid eggs in open wounds, and the eggs developed into screw worms, which caused agonizing pain—even death—to the herds. To kill the screw worms, the cowboys carried bottles of carbolic acid mixed with axle grease and rubbed the mixture into the wounds.

One cowboy was ordered to treat a bunch of cows suffering from skin mange. The standard cure was to douse the cattle with kerosene. However, one of the treated cows ran through a branding fire and turned into a living torch. The panicked cow ran back to the herd and set the whole lot afire. Twenty cattle died in the incident.

Dehorning was another unpleasant summer chore. Longhorns occasionally had to have their horns removed so they wouldn't gore each other. On most of the animals, the men cut off the horns with a saw, but the harder horns of old bulls had to be chopped off with an ax.

THE ROUNDUP

Roundups were probably the most important events that occurred on a ranch. These took place twice a year—in spring and fall. During spring roundup, cattle were brought together and counted, new calves were branded, and four- and five-year-old cows were prepared for the cattle drives. Fall roundups were mainly a mop-up of animals missed in the spring.

Spring roundup began in April or May—as soon as grass was good—and it generally took from one to two months. Cowboys from neighboring ranches joined forces to round up all the cows in a designated area. This was an enormous job because cattle were free to roam over a huge range. Some roundups covered 100 square miles.

The movement of the roundup followed the chuck wagon. Every morning after breakfast, the cowboys fanned out to gather strays. Meanwhile, the chuck wagon moved on to night camp. By late afternoon, the strays were herded to the new location for branding. Afterward, the hands had supper and bedded down for the night, taking turns guarding the herd.

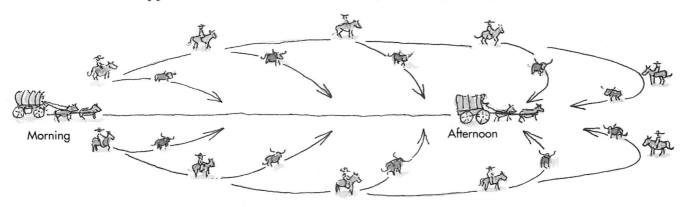

Morning

Afternoon

Once cattle had been rounded up, several experienced hands from each outfit mounted trained ponies and rode into the herd to separate, or cut, their ranch's animals. They moved slowly, looking for the owner's notch in a cow's ear. When a man identified a cow, his pony took over the job of separating it from the herd. Calves followed the mothers. Separate herds were then assembled some distance from the main herd.

Next, calves had to be separated from the older cows and branded. A skilled roper managed the first part of this task, cutting out a calf, lassoing it, and pulling it toward the branding fire. As the calf neared the fire, a second cowhand tossed a rope around its hind legs or grabbed the animal and threw it to the ground for branding.

Most cowboys wanted horses of solid colors, but no *paints*. The multi-colored paint may have been a favorite in films and fiction, but cowboys claimed that it rarely made a good cutting horse.

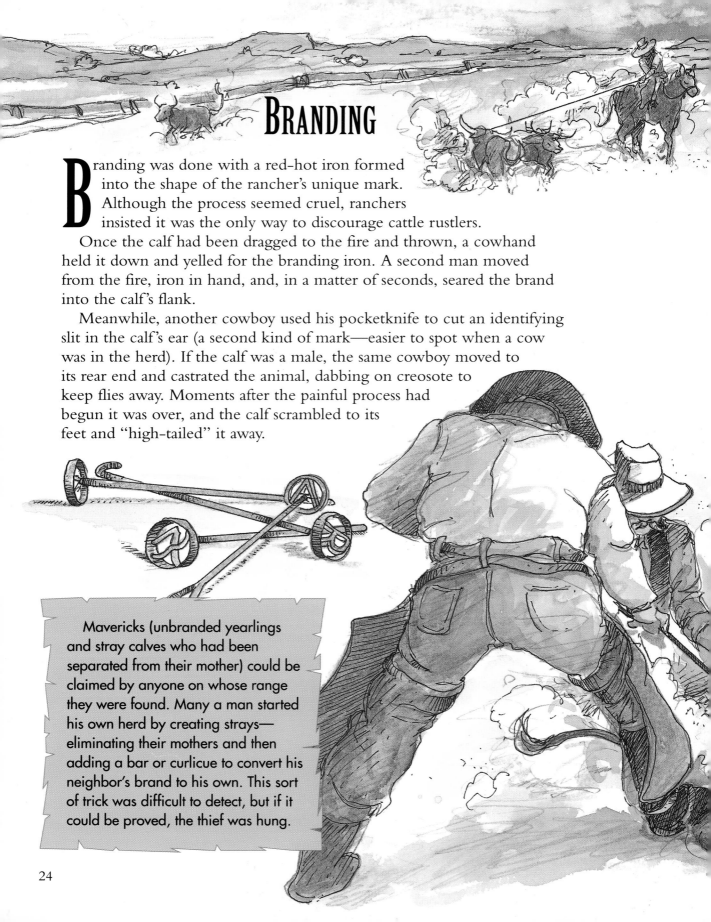

BRANDING

Branding was done with a red-hot iron formed into the shape of the rancher's unique mark. Although the process seemed cruel, ranchers insisted it was the only way to discourage cattle rustlers.

Once the calf had been dragged to the fire and thrown, a cowhand held it down and yelled for the branding iron. A second man moved from the fire, iron in hand, and, in a matter of seconds, seared the brand into the calf's flank.

Meanwhile, another cowboy used his pocketknife to cut an identifying slit in the calf's ear (a second kind of mark—easier to spot when a cow was in the herd). If the calf was a male, the same cowboy moved to its rear end and castrated the animal, dabbing on creosote to keep flies away. Moments after the painful process had begun it was over, and the calf scrambled to its feet and "high-tailed" it away.

Mavericks (unbranded yearlings and stray calves who had been separated from their mother) could be claimed by anyone on whose range they were found. Many a man started his own herd by creating strays—eliminating their mothers and then adding a bar or curlicue to convert his neighbor's brand to his own. This sort of trick was difficult to detect, but if it could be proved, the thief was hung.

Triangle

Forked Y with Double Rail

Hay Hook

Key

Tumbling Ladder

Spur

Broken Arrow

Flying 7

Diamond T

Brands were simple combinations of letters, numbers, and shapes. These and ear markings were recorded with stock associations and county courthouses as proof of ownership.

Even a greenhorn soon learned how to read a brand. The brand's elements read from left to right, from top to bottom, or from outside to inside (a T inside a diamond was read "Diamond T," not "T Diamond").

FUN AND GAMES

The roundup was hard, exhausting work. But it was also a rare chance for cowboys from different ranches to get together. Here was a time to renew old acquaintances, swap tall tales, and have a rip-snorting good time.

Many roundups began with several days of wild and woolly fun. The cowhands might hold kangaroo courts (mock trials) to pass sentence on meaningless and ridiculous offenses. A "convicted" cowboy could be sentenced to a bareback ride on a wild steer or to break a notorious bucking bronco.

Competitive sports often included roping contests, shooting matches, and horse racing. The rowdiest sport was the racing. Contestants raced between rows of standing or mounted spectators, who cheered and shot off pistols. Cowboys who had horses of their own raced each other. Whoever won got the other cowboy's horse.

At night, cowhands wandered from chuck wagon to chuck wagon, sampling specialties of the cooks, looking up old friends, and swapping yarns around the campfires.

Some of the more adventurous men sneaked off to nearby towns to drink at saloons, try out local eateries, or visit the local dance hall. Most roundups ended with a giant dance and barbecue— the big social event in the cowboys' year.

TRAIL DRIVE

The yearly trail drive was the most challenging and hazardous part of a cowboy's life. Most drives were organized by brokers who collected cattle from ranchers in Texas and delivered them to buyers in rail centers such as Abilene and Wichita. A single herd on these drives might number from 500 to 1,500 cattle, but a few had as many as 2,500.

The broker supplied a chuck wagon, a team of mules, and about 50 riding horses (often sold at the end of the drive). He provided food—coffee, sugar, bacon, dried fruit, flour, canned goods, and eggs. He paid wages to a trail boss, cook, horse wrangler, and 10 or 12 cowboys.

Drives lasted from two to four months, during which time cowboys never left the herd. They guided the cattle over rugged prairies, swam them across rivers, calmed them during fierce storms, and rounded them up after stampedes.

The Crew on a Trail Drive

The trail boss earned about $100 a month; the cook, $35 to $40; cowboys, $25 to $30; and the wrangler, $25 to $30. Each cowboy supplied his own saddle and bedroll, and occasionally his own horse. The wrangler was generally a green recruit who tended and fed the horses.

Main responsibility for the drive belonged to the trail boss, who more than earned the extra wages he was paid. It was his duty to make sure each cowboy did his job, to decide how far the outfit would move each day, and to decide where to bed down for the night. The men and animals were totally in his charge, and he was responsible for any mishaps or losses.

Upset our wagon in River & lost Many of our cooking utensils…was on my Horse the whole night & it raining hard…There was one of our party Drowned to day (Mr. Carr) & Several narrow escapes & I among [them]… Horses all give out & Men refused to do anything… Awful night… not having had a bit to eat for 60 hours… Thunder Lightning & rain—we followed our Beeves all night as they wandered about… Sick & Discouraged. Have not got the Blues but am in Hel of a fix… one man down with Boils & one with Ague… Found a Human skeleton on the Prairie to day."

—Trail boss George Duffield, 1866

29

A Long Haul

Once the drive began, each cowboy was assigned specific duties and a position to hold on the trail. The cattle were moved in a long straight line. At the head of the herd rode the trail boss—unless he chose to fall back to talk with his men. Next came the chuck wagon, pulled by mules or oxen.

Behind the chuck wagon rode veteran cowhands at the "point" positions. Their job was to lead the cattle, and they often relied on the help of a lead steer or two.

Next, the "swing" riders positioned themselves where the herd began to swell out. Further back, a pair of "flank" riders rode on each side of the herd, making sure the cattle didn't wander off. At the rear, where steers tended to bunch together, came three or more "drag" riders, young and inexperienced cowpokes who had to eat the dust kicked up by the herd.

Off to the front and side of the herd rode the remount or replacement horses (*remuda*) and the wrangler—youngest and least experienced of the cowboys—who kept them rounded up, fed, and cared for.

By mid- or late afternoon, the chuck wagon and remuda often pushed ahead to the night's campsite.

An unidentified writer in the late 1870s described the organization of a trail herd:

The ordinary order of march is the foreman [trail boss] ahead, searching for a camping place with grass and water; the drove [herd] drifting onward in the shape of a wedge, the strong few stretching out to a sharp point in front, then the line growing thicker and wider, until in the butt end is crowded the mass.

31

THE CHUCK WAGON

The chuck wagon was the cowboys' home on the trail. Before dawn, the cowboys were roused by a shout from the cook. Either they got up—*pronto*—or he'd toss their breakfast in the creek. While the cowboys ate, the cattle grazed. Then the drive moved on. Lunch came at about 11:00, supper at 5:30. After supper, the cowboys swapped tales, boasted a bit, or shot the occasional crap game—but not for long. They were bone-tired, and each had to take a two-hour shift as night guard.

Meals were monotonous: black coffee, bacon ("sowbelly"), sourdough biscuits, gravy, beans ("Pecos strawberries"), and occasionally dried prunes or apples. Cooking fires were stoked with kindling or "prairie coal"—cattle dung lit with bacon rind.

Excerpt from the trail log of a young Texan, James Bell

July 3, 1854: ...My bed is made with the...rubber coat next the ground, saddle at the head, horse blanket on the saddle to make it soft, bed blanket over all, and myself on top of that; sometimes to luxuriate a little I pull off my boots and hat. When it rains I roll up into a ball like a porcupine, and spread the gum coat over me.

Texas rancher Charles Goodnight built the first chuck wagon in 1866. To an old army wagon, he attached a large box with a lid that swung down to make a table. This chuck box held eating utensils, food supplies, medicine, whiskey, and the coffeepot.

In the wagon's bed were weapons, bedrolls, cooking utensils, grain for the mules, and tools. Strapped to one side was a water barrel, and under the wagon was a cowhide "possum-belly" to hold kindling.

The cook fixed three hot meals a day, doctored cuts, sewed buttons, and settled bets. He was the first man up and the last to retire. After the hands bedded down, he pointed the wagon's tongue toward the North Star, providing a sure compass heading come morning.

DANGERS AND HARDSHIPS ON THE DRIVE

Life on the trail was full of danger. The cowboy could be thrown from his horse, charged by an angry longhorn, or trampled in a stampede. There was no taking to his bed if he broke a leg or got sick. Few trail drives ended with the same cowboys they left with. Hands regularly quit along the way and replacements had to be hired.

It was not just the men who suffered on these long drives. Steers often went blind from lack of water during drought, drowned in flash floods or swollen rivers, died in stampedes, or became infected with disease. Many were stolen by rustlers or shot by angry homesteaders protecting their crops from the trampling herd.

Stampedes were common hazards. These occurred most frequently during storms, when cattle were spooked by sudden thunder and lightning. But stampedes were sometimes deliberately started by local townspeople or farmers, who would capture the resulting strays for themselves—or appear the next morning, offering to round up cattle for fifty cents a head.

River crossings presented some of the greatest risks on trail drives. Swollen after heavy spring rains, the raging rivers frightened cattle, horses, and cowboys alike. Men and animals faced possible drowning every time they crossed a river.

A cowboy in the late 1870s described the typical beginnings of a stampede:

The first symptom of alarm is snorting. Then, if the guards are numerous and alert, so that the cattle cannot easily break away, they will begin "milling", i.e., crowding together with their heads toward a common center, their horns clashing, and the whole body in confused rotary motion, which increases, and unless controlled, ends in a concentrated outbreak and stampede.

35

The End of the Trail

For the cowboys, it must have seemed like the trail drive would never end. But finally, one of the men would spot—rising up like a mirage—the town they'd been headed for all those weeks.

Once the herd had been quieted, cattle were led into pens, sold, and loaded on railroad cars for the trip to slaughterhouses. The cowboys' work was finally over. Each hand was given his pay. With hoots and hollers, the cowpokes headed for town. The first stop for many was a barbershop where they laid out $1.25 for a shave and haircut and two bits more ($.25) for a hot bath. The next stop was generally the closest saloon.

During the long months of the drive, the cowboy had had very little money and no place to spend it. Suddenly he felt rich. And in every cattle town were saloon keepers, dance hall women, and gamblers eager to help him spend his money. As an Old West newspaper reporter described it:

For the matter of a week, or perchance two—it depends on how fast his money melts—in these fashions will our gentleman of cows engage his hours and expand himself. He will make a deal of noise, drink a deal of whiskey, acquire a deal of what he terms "action"; but he harms nobody, and, in a town toughened to his racket and which needs and gets his money, disturbs nobody.

Finally, after their spree had ended, the cowboys drifted out of town with just enough money—if they were lucky—to catch a train or steamboat back to Texas. A veteran cowboy remembered his return:

I always had the "big time" when I arrived in San Antonio rigged out with a pair of high-heeled boots and striped pants and about $6.30 worth of other clothes…I would soon be busted and have to borrow money to get out to the ranch, where I would put in the fall and winter telling about the big things I had seen up North. The next spring I would have the same old trip, the same old things would happen in the same old way, and with the same old wind-up. I put in eighteen or twenty years on the trail and all I had in the final outcome was the high-heeled boots, the striped pants, and about $4.80 worth of other clothes, so there you are.

WINTER ON THE RANCH

The quietest time around a ranch was winter. By late November, two of every three hands had been laid off. Cowboys who remained had the grueling winter task of making sure cattle weren't starving or freezing to death. Bundled in bulky buffalo coats, they rode out to find hillsides free of snow and then drove the cattle to these spots to graze. The cowboys often had to chop through snow and ice so cattle could drink. At other times, the cowboys collected firewood or hunted prairie wolves that preyed on the cattle.

Many cowboys spent winter in town, painting houses, tending bar, or blacksmithing. Others survived by "grub-line riding" from ranch to ranch—picking up free meals in exchange for odd jobs.

The Bunkhouse

A cowboy's ranch home was the bunkhouse, usually a shack of weatherboard or cottonwood logs. Every bunkhouse smelled of sweat, dry cow manure, chewing tobacco, old boots, and smoke from oil lamps. There was a uniform untidiness to the places, too. To most cowboys, life in the bunkhouse was a constant battle against filth and boredom.

On hot summer evenings, cowboys often bedded out on the ground rather than sharing the hot, crowded bunkhouse with bedbugs and gray backs (body lice). One cowpuncher recalled that his bunkmates "made an iron-clad rule that whoever was caught picking gray backs off and throwing them on the floor without first killing them, should pay a fine of ten cents for each and every offense."

Bunkhouse winters were even worse. After one winter at a ranch in Texas, cowboy Harry Ingerton pronounced the bunkhouse "the coldest place I ever saw." The few blankets available did not help much. "If I owned a ranch," grumbled cowhand Peter Wright, "I'd buy these blankets and use them as a refrigerator in the summer."

THE END OF THE COWBOY YEARS

By the end of the 1880s, open-range cattle ranching had collapsed. Too many animals had overgrazed the ranges. Overproduction of beef had driven cattle prices down. Farmers and sheepherders were competing with ranchers for land. And the final blow was dealt by Mother Nature: a bitterly cold winter in 1885 was followed by a summer drought that withered the grass and dried up all the streams. The next winter brought snows so deep cattle couldn't get to the grass. After the blizzards came record cold—with temperatures dipping as low as 60 degrees below zero.

"When spring finally came," wrote historian Ray Allen Billington, "cattlemen saw a sight they spent the rest of their lives trying to forget. Carcass piled upon carcass in every ravine, gaunt skeletons staggering about on frozen feet, trees stripped bare of their bark…" The day of the open range had ended. The Golden Age of the cowboy was over.

But the image of the cowboy lives on. It has been preserved—in more glamorous, romantic form—in our legends, songs, movies, and novels. And glimpses of the old cowboy are reflected in the lives of men and women who ride the ranges today.

Perhaps the best, truest summary of the great American cowboy was captured in these words of a present-day Texas cowhand:

I'll tell you what a cowpuncher is… It ain't roping and it ain't riding bronc and it ain't being smart, neither. It's thinking enough about a dumb animal to go out in the rain or snow to try to save that cow. Not for the guy who owns the cow but for the poor old cow and her calf. It's getting down in that bog—in the quicksand… You tie up one leg, then the other. You tramp her out… You see, this old cow, she don't know but what you're trying to kill her. But you drag her out, even if she's fighting you, and then you ride a mile yonder and find another danged old cow bogged down the same way.

TRAIL MUSIC

Many cowboy songs and ballads were composed for cows. The songs helped calm the cattle—especially on stormy nights—as they were sung by cowhands circling the herd during night guard duty. The rhythm of the music was often set by the gait of the cowhand's horse.

from "The Old Chisholm Trail"

I'm up in the mornin' afore daylight
And afore I sleep the moon shines bright.

No chaps and no slicker, and it's pouring down rain,
And I swear, by God, that I'll never night-herd again.

Oh, it's bacon and beans most every day—
I'd as soon be a'eatin' prairie hay.

I went to the boss to draw my roll,
He had it figured out I was nine dollars in the hole.

I'll sell my horse and I'll sell my saddle;
You can go to hell with your longhorn cattle.

from "Get Along, Little Dogies"

Early in the spring we round up the dogies,
Mark 'em and brand 'em and bob off their tails;
Drive up our horses, load up the chuck wagon,
then throw the dogies out on the trail.

Oh, some boys go up the trail for pleasure,
But that's where they gets it most awfully wrong;
For you have no idea the trouble they give us,
While we go a-driving them along.

TRAIL RECIPES

The three recipes below are similar to ones used by cooks on western cattle drives and roundups.

Cowboy Beans

2 pounds of pinto beans
2-pound ham hock or salt pork
2 chopped onions

4 tablespoons sugar
1 jalapeño pepper, seeded and diced
1 can tomato paste

Rinse the beans and soak them in water overnight. Drain, place beans in a Dutch oven, and add water to cover. Add the remaining ingredients and simmer at low heat until tender (for about an hour). Sample while cooking and add salt to taste and water as needed.

Sourdough Biscuits

1 cup sourdough starter
1 teaspoon each of salt, sugar, baking soda

2 tablespoons shortening
3 to 4 cups sifted flour

Place 3 cups flour in bowl, make a well in center, and add sourdough starter (recipe follows). Stir in salt, soda, and sugar. Add 1 tablespoon shortening. Gradually mix in enough flour to make a stiff dough. Pinch off dough for one biscuit at a time. Form piece of dough into a ball and roll it in 1 tablespoon melted shortening. Crowd the biscuits in a round 8-inch cake pan and allow to rise in a warm place for 20 to 30 minutes before baking. Bake at 425° for 10 to 15 minutes or until golden brown. Makes 15 to 20 biscuits.

Sourdough Starter

2 potatoes, peeled and cubed
3 cups water

2 cups flour
1 tablespoon sugar

Boil potatoes in 3 cups water until tender. Remove potatoes and measure out 2 cups of the liquid. Mix potato water with flour and sugar to make a smooth paste. Set in a warm place until this mixture doubles its original size. Store in an airtight container in refrigerator.

TRUE-LIFE COWBOYS

Charles Siringo was born in Texas in 1856. As a young man, Siringo signed on as a cowhand for a stingy cattle baron. His first job was to round up 1,100 longhorns and help an inexperienced cattle buyer drive them to Kansas. The entire herd got away from the new owner's crew and wandered back home. There, the cattle baron rounded them up and sold them again. In 1874 Siringo signed on with a trail drive, receiving $35 a month, plus a railroad ticket back home. Once on the trail, however, he fell out with the trail boss. Siringo was a crack bronco buster, and whenever he'd broken a wild horse, the boss gave it to a less skilled rider and found Siringo another bronco to bust. Fed up and saddle sore, Siringo quit. Years later, after countless exciting adventures, Siringo became a range detective, tracking down cattle thieves. He died in 1928 after writing several books about his adventures, including the popular autobiography, *A Texas Cow Boy or, Fifteen Years on the Hurricane Deck of a Spanish Pony*.

Nat Love was the most famous African-American cowboy. Born in a Tennessee slave cabin in 1854, Love headed for Kansas after the Civil War. When he arrived in Dodge City at 15, Love was invited to have breakfast with a Texas trail outfit. When he asked for a job with the men, the trail boss had him prove his skill by riding a wild horse. Love described "his test ride": "I thought I had rode pitching horses before, but from the moment I mounted Good Eye I knew I had not learned what pitching was. This proved the worst horse to ride I had ever mounted…but I stayed with him and the cowboys were the most surprised outfit you ever saw, as they had taken me for a tenderfoot, pure and simple." Love got the job and worked as a cowboy until 1890. His skill as a horseman—proved in a riding contest at Deadwood, Dakota Territory—earned him the nickname "Deadwood Dick." Love's autobiography, *The Life and Adventures of Nat Love*, was published in 1907.

Buck Taylor—known as the "King of the Cowboys"—was the first cowboy star of Buffalo Bill Cody's famous Wild West show. William Levi "Buck" Taylor was born near Fredericksburg, Texas, in 1857. Orphaned at the age of six, Taylor spent his childhood and teenage years on ranches in Texas. He later drifted north to Nebraska, where he hired on at William Cody's North Platte Ranch. When he joined Cody's Wild West show, Taylor had more than mastered the toughest cowboy skills. The show's programs described him as "amiable as a child" but claimed that Taylor could throw a steer by the horns and tie it single-handed, snatch a handkerchief off the ground while on the back of a galloping horse, and ride the wildest bucking broncos.

Cowboy Terms and their Meaning

bronco (Spanish for "wild, rough"): any wiry, spirited horse

buckaroo (from Spanish *vaquero*—"cow herder"): cowboy

chaps (from Spanish *chaparro prieto*—the thorny, tangled brush that gave the South Texas chaparral country its name): leather leggings worn over pants as protection from thorny bushes

chuck: cowboy word for "food." The chuck wagon carried food and cooking supplies.

cinch (from Spanish *cincha*—"a girth"): wide band that circles a horse's belly to hold the saddle in place

corral: Spanish word for a pen or enclosure for horses or livestock

cowpoke, cowpuncher: slang terms that cowhands used for one another. "Cowpuncher" came from the cowhand's use of a long pole to urge cows into cattle cars. "Cowpokes" stuck similar poles through the sides of the cattle cars to make reclining cows stand up so they wouldn't be trampled.

cutting: riding into a herd to separate selected cows or steers

dogies: orphaned young cattle; any young steers

drag rider: on a trail drive, the cowboy who rode at the rear of the herd

drover: one who drives cattle or sheep, often the trail boss

dude: term for an "overcivilized" dandy—often from the East—who played at being a cowboy

flank rider: trail-drive cowboy who rode alongside the herd, keeping cows from straying off

greenhorn: any new, inexperienced cowhand. The term possibly originated because the cowhand's wooden saddle horn was still new ("green").

grub-line riding: riding from ranch to ranch doing odd jobs in exchange for food ("grub")

lariat (from Spanish *la reata*—"the rope"): a cowboy's rope, used to lasso steers

maverick: any unbranded stray animal, especially a cow or horse

mustang (from Spanish *mesteño*—"stray"): Spanish word for the wild broncos of Texas and New Mexico

point rider: trail-drive cowboy who rode at the head of the herd

poke: leather purse in which a cowboy carried his money

rancheros: Spanish for "ranchers"

remuda (Spanish word meaning "replacement"): the herd of spare horses or remounts handled by the wrangler

riding herd: riding around a herd of cattle to keep it together and guard it

rodeo (from Spanish *rodear*—"to surround"): a cowboy circus with roping and riding competition

swing rider: trail-drive cowboy who rode back from the head of the herd, where the line of cattle began to thicken and swell

taps (from Spanish *tapaderos*—"covers"): the hood over a stirrup that protected the rider's foot from thorns

tenderfoot: any greenhorn; first applied to eastern cattle that were shipped west for breeding

wrangler (from Spanish *caballerango*—"horse herdsman"): usually the least experienced cowhand on a trail drive whose job was to look after the remuda

INDEX

Robert Klausmeier is an editor and writer living in St. Paul, Minnesota. He traces his avid interest in cowboys to a childhood filled with Roy Rogers and Hopalong Cassidy films and the Lone Ranger serial on the radio.

Richard Erickson graduated from Atlanta's Portfolio Center in 1989. A native of Chicago, he currently lives in the North Georgia Mountains with his wife Kathy, two sons, four dogs, and three cats.